Waiting in Joyful Hope

*Daily Reflections for
Advent and Christmas
2012–2013*

SO-CFH-925

Jay Cormier

LITURGICAL PRESS

Collegeville, Minnesota

www.litpress.org

Nihil Obstat: Reverend Robert Harren, *Censor deputatus.*
Imprimatur: ✠ Most Reverend John F. Kinney, J.C.D., D.D., Bishop of St. Cloud, Minnesota, May 11, 2012.

Cover design by Ann Blattner. Photo: Top Photo Group/Thinkstock.

ISSN 1550-803X

ISBN 978-0-8146-3362-5

Introduction

John was sent from God . . . to testify to the light, so that all
might believe through him. . . .

[John] saw Jesus coming toward him and said, "Behold,
the Lamb of God, who takes away the sin of the world. He is
the one of whom I said, 'A man is coming after me who ranks
ahead of me because he existed before me.' I did not know
him, but the reason why I came baptizing with water was
that he might be made known to Israel." (John 1:6-7, 29-31)

Every December, John the Baptist makes his appearance in
our Advent Scripture readings, proclaiming the coming of
the Christ and calling us to "prepare his way" by prayer and
penance.

On the Sundays of Advent, we hear the Synoptic Gospels'
portrait of John: the eccentric figure clad in camel skins sur-
viving on locusts and wild honey, who severely criticizes the
religious establishment for their faithlessness and challenges
all who dare approach him to embrace his baptism of repentance and conversion.

But after Christmas, in the readings from the Fourth Gospel, we see a very different image of John. In the gospels read
in late December and early January, the evangelist John presents a much more approachable Baptizer: a serene, compassionate, reconciling figure who bridges the age of the
prophets and the dawning of the Messiah. The writer of the
Fourth Gospel presents John as a voice of hope and joy who
dedicates himself to giving testimony to the "light." The
self-effacing John of the Fourth Gospel goes to great lengths

to minimize his role in order to enable the people of the Jordan region to recognize the Christ walking among them. In the Fourth Gospel, the Baptizer is the welcoming entryway for many to behold the Lamb of God in their midst. John opens the hearts and spirits of those who come to his baptism to the first light and hope of the Messiah.

The reflections in this year's edition of *Waiting in Joyful Hope* take their cue from the John the Baptizer of the Fourth Gospel. The stories and images in the pages that follow reflect Advent's call to discover the compassion, peace, and justice of God in our midst and enable others to behold the presence of Emmanuel ("God with us") in their lives as well. This season of Advent challenges us to take up God's call for us to be prophets of his Messiah: to straighten the crooked roads of our lives, to transform "deserts" barren of love into places of welcome and reconciliation, to gather up the lost and forgotten, and to proclaim the coming of God's Christ in our midst.

This Christmas, may you add your own voice to that of John to proclaim the constant presence of God in our midst. May the love and kindness you extend this Christmas reflect the light of Christ who dawns in this holy season and illuminates every season of every year with his peace.

FIRST WEEK OF ADVENT

To Stand Before Jesus

Readings: Jer 33:14-16; 1 Thess 3:12–4:2; Luke 21:25-28, 34-36

Scripture:
"But when these signs begin to happen,
stand erect and raise your heads
because your redemption is at hand." (Luke 21:28)

Reflection: Time is up. No turning back, no second chances, no retakes. It is over. Done. Finished.

Now you find yourself standing before Jesus, face-to-face. The Jesus you received so many times in the eucharistic bread and wine. The Jesus you professed belief in every Sunday. The Jesus you called on in countless panic-driven prayers. The Jesus whose very name—*Christ*—you took on in baptism.

And now you stand before him.

Jesus holds no record book of your life, no scales of justice. There is no laser-intense gaze, no threats, no instant condemnations.

Jesus says nothing.

There is nothing to be said. Jesus knows you in the deepest recesses of your heart.

So what do you say? What do you do? Will that moment be filled with terror? Will you be overcome, as was Peter in the gospel, with the number of times you betrayed him in your anger, in your hatred, in your selfishness, in your obtuseness to those around you? Will you shrink before Jesus, unable to stand before him? You may want to run and hide, but there will be no place to go.

Or will you be able to muster up all the courage you have to say humbly to Jesus, *I did my best. Thank you.*

And Jesus will say, *I know. And you're welcome.*

And then Jesus will welcome you like an old friend, with a big hug, into the eternal dwelling place of his Father.

In his gospel, Luke portrays our final judgment very simply: "to stand before the Son of Man." But rather than make us tremble, the prospect of standing before Jesus should fill us with hope: that the "shoot of Jesse" comes to redeem us and lead us through the darkest nights, the most perilous storms, the most tumultuous calamities we will face in our lives. These four weeks of Advent are a microcosm of the Advent that is the very entirety of lives as Christians: to be ready "to stand before the Son of Man" through lives of love, mercy, and justice.

Meditation: What would you like to be able to say to Jesus at the moment when you meet him? How can this Advent be a time for preparing your words?

Prayer: Come, Lord Jesus, into this Advent of our lives with your justice and mercy. May we welcome you with hearts humbled by gratitude for the very gift of life we have been given; may we behold you in every sign of your love and forgiveness in our midst.

December 3: Monday of the First Week of Advent

Every Precious Advent Moment

Readings: Isa 2:1-5; Matt 8:5-11

Scripture:
The centurion said [to Jesus] in reply,
"Lord, I am not worthy to have you enter under my roof;
only say the word and my servant will be healed." (Matt 8:8)

Reflection: Anyone who has lived with cancer or has survived a cardiac event or has conquered some debilitating disease will tell you the same thing: every tick of your watch, every second that flashes by on your desk clock, every hour of every day is precious.

They will explain how you prize family and friends, how quickly you understand that they are as scared and confused as you are. Every walk in the woods becomes an encounter with the sacred. Every moment spent with your spouse and children and grandchildren and friends is treasured. Time is too precious to waste on recriminations and pettiness, on judgments and rejections. Even though you are the one in need of compassion, you develop the rare ability to offer consolation and support to friends and loved ones.

Every choice you make is with great care—from what you will have for dinner to what book you will read. Joy, peace, reconciliation, and serenity are the driving forces in your life. There is no time to waste on quarreling or fighting old wars.

Once you realize that your exit from life's stage has been set, once you accept the reality that "later" is "now" and "tomorrow" is "today," every moment is savored, every love is cherished, every experience is lived to the fullest, with gratitude and joy.

This season of Advent calls us to realize what the chronically and terminally ill come to understand: that the gift of time—which we so often take for granted—is precious and limited, that our lives constantly change and turn and are transformed, that we have much to do in the short time we have been given. God gives us this lifetime in order that we might rediscover him in the love of others and in the goodness of this world in anticipation of the next. Every day of our lives is an Advent of hope, expectation, and preparation—an Advent in which a Roman army officer dares to hope in the healing powers of a Jewish teacher; an Advent of rediscovering the presence of God in the midst of all our joys and sorrows, in the midst of our fears and brokenness, in the midst of our regrets and healings.

Meditation: When did you realize your own mortality? How did that experience affect your appreciation of life?

Prayer: Come, O Christ, Healer and Worker of Wonders. May we trust in your Word to heal our afflictions and illnesses; may we hope in your light to shatter the darkness of our despair and pain. Let us live the Advent of our lives with faith in your compassion and hope in your grace.

Discovering the Limits

Readings: Isa 11:1-10; Luke 10:21-24

Scripture:
"I give you praise, Father, Lord of heaven and earth,
for although you have hidden these things
from the wise and learned
you have revealed them to the childlike." (Luke 10:21)

Reflection: It was Tom's first day. Looking for his sixth-grade classroom, he asked directions from a boy walking by. The boy quietly pointed to Tom's room, not smiling or looking at him. Tom thanked him and took his place at his desk.

At recess Tom caught up with him. His name was Kyle and he was in the sixth grade as well. They talked about the stuff that sixth-graders talk about. At one point, Kyle almost smiled. They met after school, shot some baskets, and got some Cokes. Kyle asked about the MP3 player Tom had in his backpack; when Kyle put in the earbuds and listened to the music, it was the only genuine smile he showed. Tom stood in awe of Kyle's skill on the court—Kyle seemed to be able to sink the ball perfectly from anywhere, at will. Kyle showed Tom how to gauge his shots more accurately.

That evening, Tom's parents asked how the first day went. OK, he said. He liked his teachers for the most part, lunch was all right, and he met this new kid. A look of concern immediately came over their faces when Tom mentioned

Kyle's name. Maybe Tom better steer clear of Kyle, they suggested. There were stories about his family . . . his father never seemed to be around . . . one of Kyle's brothers has a long record . . . didn't they live in the projects?

But what did that have to do with Kyle? Tom wondered. He's a good kid. Still, Mom and Dad said, they'd feel more comfortable if Tom didn't spend too much time with Kyle.

The next day at school, Kyle was the first to see Tom. "Hi," Kyle said, with an easiness that wasn't there yesterday.

"Hey," Tom said, but kept walking. Tom never spent any more time with Kyle. And Tom never really told his parents anymore about school. Or anything else that mattered.

Christ calls us to embrace the genuine faith of a child that we adults sadly "outgrow." "Child-like faith" is never discouraged, never becomes cynical or jaded, never ceases to be amazed and grateful for the many ways God reveals his presence. The power of such faith is its ability to overcome every fear, complication, and agenda in order to mirror the selflessness, integrity, and generosity of Christ Jesus.

Meditation: When have you found the words of Jesus at odds with the wisdom or expectations of those around you?

Prayer: As we anticipate your coming to us a humble child this Christmas, Lord Jesus, help us to embrace your gospel with simple, childlike faith—faith that is profound in its total commitment to imitating your Spirit of understanding compassion, faith that is focused on making your Father's kingdom of reconciling peace a reality in our time and place.

"Sacramental" Holiday Shopping

Readings: Isa 25:6-10a; Matt 15:29-37

Scripture:
Then he took the seven loaves and the fish,
gave thanks, broke the loaves,
and gave them to the disciples, who in turn gave them to
the crowds.
They all ate and were satisfied. (Matt 15:36-37)

Reflection: The story of Jesus feeding the crowds is the only miracle of Jesus that is recorded in all four gospels. The early church cherished this story—they saw the story as precursor to Jesus' institution of the Eucharist.

In all the gospel accounts, the miracle begins with an act of giving. Before Jesus can take, bless, and break the loaves and fish, somebody has to come forward and offer the few scraps they have. In Matthew's version (today's gospel), when confronted with the large number of hungry people, Jesus asks the disciples what they have to give. All they are able to collect are seven loaves and "a few fish." With that, Jesus performs the miracle.

As we are about to go full bore into our Christmas shopping, keep this story in mind. If we give what we have and are, regardless of how little and insignificant it might seem, it can be a Christlike expression of love. Just as Jesus takes what little the disciples can come up with and feeds the thousands of poor, sick, and suffering who have come to him, we can make our own small miracles by imitating his example of taking from our want, blessing it in gratitude to the God who gave it to us, and giving it lovingly and generously. Even the smallest gifts we give this Christmas season—if given out of love and the desire to bring joy and enrichment to the recipient—can be as sacramental as the loaves and fish Jesus gives on the mountainside by Galilee.

This Advent, may our gift giving be small but effective miracles of God's love in our midst.

Meditation: In what specific ways can the story of the miracle of the loaves and fish inspire your Christmas shopping this year?

Prayer: Lord Jesus, may your compassion be the gift we give this Christmas. Take the pieces of bread and fish that we are able to give and transform them into sacraments of your compassion for those we love. May we work "miracles" of generosity and forgiveness through which our families and communities may rediscover your loving presence in our midst.

On the Street Where You Live

Readings: Isa 26:1-6; Matt 7:21, 24-27

Scripture:
"Everyone who listens to these words of mine and acts on
  them
will be like the wise man who built his house on rock."
  (Matt 7:24)

Reflection: Two houses stand across from each other on the same neighborhood street.

The first house is right out of *Architectural Digest*. The yard is professionally landscaped; the manicured lawn would be the envy of any golf course. Expensive automobiles are parked in the driveway. Fine brocade and silk border the windows; the rooms are filled with elegant furniture and antiques. Everything is immaculate—from the wine cellar in the basement to the master suite upstairs.

The second house is not a dump but hardly a magazine cover. Bicycles, ball games, and wading pools have pockmarked the lawn. The driveway is strewn with toys and sports equipment of all kinds. A durable van and sensible car, both with lots of miles and dents, are parked in the driveway. The house is decorated in a style that can most charitably be described as "eclectic." Everyone has chores to perform, but keeping everything clean and neat is a challenge.

In the first house, it is always quiet, its inhabitants like ships passing in the night. The parents are away on business; the son and daughter have their own schedules, friends, and activities. Four separate lives exist in the first house.

But there is always something going on in the second house. Schoolwork, games, and projects of all kinds light up every room. The menu is simple, but everyone pitches in to help.

While cold formality chills the interior of the first house, love, compassion, forgiveness, and support make the second house into a real home.

The parable of the house built on rock resonates during this Christmas season when we are especially aware of our families and loved ones. Our homes are meant to be safe places of compassion and forgiveness, "stables" where the love of God is reborn every day. Sometimes that love is spoken in near-perfect joy; at other times, that love cries out in desperate pain. Renewed by the joy of Christmas, may we be the reassuring and comforting love of Christ for one another in every season of the year.

Meditation: In what ways do you sense the presence of God dwelling in your home?

Prayer: O God, be the rock on which we build our lives. May we welcome you as the always-present, unseen Guest in our homes and at our tables. By your wisdom and grace, may we build dwellings of love and forgiveness, homes where your Spirit of love is the hearth that warms our hearts.

Restoring Hope in the Desert of Avarice

Readings: Isa 29:17-24; Matt 9:27-31

Scripture:
When he entered the house,
the blind men approached him and Jesus said to them,
"Do you believe that I can do this?"
"Yes, Lord," they said to him.
Then he touched their eyes and said,
"Let it be done for you according to your faith."
  (Matt 9:28-29)

Reflection: Charles Dickens's *A Christmas Carol* is arguably, after the gospel narratives of Jesus' birth, the best-known and most-beloved story of the Christmas season.

In his encounters with the three Christmas ghosts, Ebenezer Scrooge confronts the cynicism that has engulfed his life. In his singular pursuit of wealth and position, Scrooge has lost family, friends, and faith. Scrooge is unable to hope in anything; he believes in nothing but the figures in his ledger.

In a poignant scene, the Ghost of Christmas Past revisits the young Scrooge's last meeting with his beloved Belle, who had come to realize that they would never marry. "There was an eager, greedy, restless motion in [Scrooge's] eye, which showed the passion that had taken root."

Despite the young Scrooge's protests, Belle knows that her beloved Ebenezer has changed. "If you were free today, tomorrow, yesterday, can even I believe you would choose a dowerless girl—you who, in your very confidence with her, weigh everything by Gain: or, choosing her, if for a moment you were false enough to your one guiding principle to do so, do I not know that your repentance and regret would surely follow?"

Watching his younger self destroy his relationship with this gentle, wise young woman, the older Scrooge begins to realize what has become of his life.

Today's gospel reading recounts two blind men who, despite their physical challenge, have found reason to hope in this Jesus—a hope that Scrooge has lost to his avarice but will rediscover this Christmas night. Over the course of our years, we lose the optimism of youth and become mired in cynicism; we replace our idealism with idols of wealth and self-interest; the hard realities of making a living slowly destroy our dreams of living a life of meaning and purpose.

Let the light of Christ illuminate our vision so that we may realize the possibilities we have to remake our lives in compassion and gratitude.

Meditation: What hopes and dreams would you like to rekindle this Christmas?

Prayer: O healing Christ, come into our hearts and homes this Advent. Open our eyes to the light of your compassion; restore our tired spirits so that we may hope again in the possibilities of resurrection in the brokenness of our lives.

December 8:
Immaculate Conception of the Blessed Virgin Mary

"The Luck of Roaring Camp"

Readings: Gen 3:9-15, 20; Eph 1:3-6, 11-12; Luke 1:26-38

Scripture:
"Behold, you will conceive in your womb and bear a son,
and you shall name him Jesus.
He will be great and will be called Son of the Most High."
(Luke 1:31-32)

Reflection: In his volumes of short stories, Bret Hart chronicled the real American Wild West: the characters who built this country in the frontier beyond the Mississippi in the late eighteenth century. In one of his stories, "The Luck of Roaring Camp," a pregnant, sick Indian woman stumbles into a camp of gruff, hard-drinking, fierce prospectors. Two of the men suddenly find themselves in the alien world of midwifery. Although the mother dies, her child, a boy, survives.

Deaths were common in Roaring Camp, but a birth was something entirely new. Immediately, the men of Roaring Camp assume responsibility for the boy, taking turns caring for him. They build a cabin, not a makeshift shack but "clean, boarded and papered"—complete with lace curtains! As they care for the boy, they begin to shed their roughness and cool their tempers. They see the world as much larger than their own dreams of gold. To hold the child or sing to him is considered a privilege and sacred trust. They demand from one another such previously unheard of things as cleanliness, quiet, and civility. They come to consider the child not a burden but a gift—and name him "Luck," Thomas Luck.

Little Thomas Luck transforms the outpost of rough, crude miners into a community of generosity, tenderness, and compassion. The child brings forth from these reckless characters and criminals dignity, humility, and a sense of beauty, wonder, and joy. An old frontier expression takes on new meaning for Roaring Camp: "The luck was with them."

Christ has come—the very Word and Light of God dwells in our midst. In his birth, we are reborn; in his humanity, our humanity is made sacred; in his life, God touches all of human history with compassion, joy, and peace.

Today, we honor Mary's "immaculate conception"—her call from God to bring the God-Child into our world. The Eastern church honors Mary as *Theotokos*—"Bearer of God." May we come to realize our call to bring God into our own time and place, to be "bearers of God," that our generosity, caring, and forgiveness may transform the Roaring Camps and Nazareths around us.

Meditation: How does the celebration of Jesus' birth each December impact the other months and seasons of your life?

Prayer: Gracious God, may we possess the faith and trust of your daughter Mary to welcome your Christ into our midst. May his birth illuminate our homes and hearts and transform our lives into worthy dwelling places of your compassion and peace.

SECOND WEEK OF ADVENT

The Work of the Baptizer

Readings: Bar 5:1-9; Phil 1:4-6, 8-11, Luke 3:1-6

Scripture:
John went throughout the whole region of the Jordan, proclaiming a baptism of repentance for the forgiveness of sins. (Luke 3:3)

Reflection: 'Tis the busy season for Santa Claus and Kris Kringle.

We are all working very hard to be Santa for those we love—or to be good enough for Santa to come down our chimney this Christmas with that perfect gift.

We may be someone's Kris Kringle or "secret Santa" this season, having chosen a member of our family or classmate or fellow worker for whom we will try to make this Christmas a little more special and happy. Being Santa or Kris Kringle can be hard but fulfilling work; we can receive as much as we give in our Santa-playing.

But every Advent our gospel readings center on this strange, austere, humorless character, John the Baptizer. The John who subsists on locusts and wild honey, clad in camel hair, haunting a wild river bank is no one's idea of Christmas joy. We happily take on the role of Kris Kringle, but no way do we see ourselves as John the Baptizer.

But that is exactly who Advent calls us to be. In our own baptisms we promised to become Baptizers along our own Jordan Rivers. So let's take on the work of the "Baptizer" this Christmas; let's become heralds like John as we go about our holiday preparations: May every kindness and generosity we extend this Christmas mirror Christ's presence in our midst. May we joyfully take on the hard work of creating a highway through the rugged lands of estrangement and alienation. May the gifts and greetings and hospitality we extend proclaim the good news that God's compassion has dawned.

Meditation: What crooked road can you straighten this Christmas? How can your Christmas celebration proclaim Christ in our midst?

Prayer: Redeeming God, may we take up this Christmas the work of your herald John: straightening the crooked roads of our lives, transforming "deserts" barren of love into places of welcome and reconciliation, gathering up the lost and forgotten, proclaiming the coming of your Christ into our homes and hearts.

December 10: Monday of the Second Week of Advent

Lessons of History

Readings: Isa 35:1-10; Luke 5:17-26

Scripture:
"Which is easier, to say, 'Your sins are forgiven,'
or to say, 'Rise and walk'?" (Luke 5:23)

Reflection: The professor assigned his U.S. history seminar students a ten-page research paper on Thomas Jefferson, due at the end of the semester.

One student went to work that night. Schoolwork did not come easily to him so he had to work hard to keep up. He was a history major and his dream was to be a high school history teacher. Over the next few weeks he spent hours reading, making notes, and rewriting his draft. He got a C. He made an appointment with the professor. The professor showed him both the strengths and weaknesses of the paper, where his analysis was faulty, what facts he failed to grasp. The student rewrote the paper and got his grade up to a B+.

Another student in the course was a member of a fraternity. One of the great perks of membership was access to an archive of research papers written by students over the years, so the second student took a couple of papers, cut and pasted as needed, and submitted the paper. His grade: A-.

Now, the obvious moral here is that the first student learned more than the second student from the research assignment.

But the first student learned much more than Jeffersonian democracy. He learned how to *learn*, how to think, how to reason. He was willing to fail in order to succeed.

The second student got a good grade in a course he quickly forgot about.

The experience of the two students mirrors the point of today's gospel. With the help of his generous and compassionate friends, a paralyzed man comes to Jesus to be healed—but instead, Jesus (to the outrage of those who witness the event) forgives the paralytic his sins. Feeling better is the "easy A"; but to heal the brokenness of the soul and spirit, to treat the illness of our own sin and self-centeredness, to mend torn relationships is to actually "write the paper," and in the process become fully alive and whole. To be able to "pick up our mats" and walk is one thing—but God has called us to live in the light of his compassion and grace, regardless of our abilities or limitations. Faith challenges us not to be satisfied with easy grades and merely feeling better but to take on the hard work of learning and seeking spiritual wholeness.

Meditation: When have you found the "quick fix" unsatisfying in the long term?

Prayer: Christ our Redeemer, help us to take on the demanding work of reconciliation. Do not let us be satisfied with quick fixes or simply feeling better but by your grace may we persevere in healing relationships and dealing with those fears and hurts that have paralyzed us spiritually.

December 11: Tuesday of the Second Week of Advent

The Limits of "Good" Shepherding

Readings: Isa 40:1-11; Matt 18:12-14

Scripture:
"If a man has a hundred sheep and one of them goes
    astray,
will he not leave the ninety-nine in the hills
and go in search of the stray?" (Matt 18:12-14)

Reflection: Would someone who had a hundred sheep *really* leave the ninety-nine and go in search of one missing sheep?

Actually, Jesus, he probably would *not*.

There comes a time to cut your losses. There are some sheep who are always getting lost. You could destroy your own life and the lives of your other "sheep" if you're constantly spending your time bringing back this one irresponsible, self-absorbed sheep.

We all have "lost" sheep in our lives: They monopolize our attention, usurp our energy, and demand more of our time than they are reasonably entitled to. They anger us, frustrate us, and sometimes even turn on us.

Point taken, Jesus would say. But that's the difficult thing about discipleship. As God constantly seeks us out and brings us back, we are called to do the same. Jesus asks us to "hang tough" with them, not to reject them or move on without them, because everyone is precious and "worth it" in the eyes of God. Such "shepherding" often demands infinite patience and understanding that can be overwhelming in its demands. And sometimes it requires "tough" love on our parts. But writing someone off completely, letting a lost soul perish in the hills, is not an option for the disciple.

God throws away no one; God does not write off anyone as hopeless or irredeemable. Even the most "little," the least promising, the slowest and struggling are beloved by God. Christ promises us the grace and strength to keep seeking the lost among us and rejoice in their recovery, their conversion, their "being found."

Meditation: Is there a "stray" in your life who demands more from you than you are able to give, who takes advantage of your generosity and sympathy? Or a "little one" whose struggles and need for assistance exhaust your patience and resources to help?

Prayer: Gracious God, give us the patience and wisdom to find a way to bring back the lost sheep in our lives, to care for the "little ones" in our midst. Illuminate our perspective with the grace of humility so that we may see those considered "little" as our brothers and sisters. May we always remember that in serving them, we serve you; in seeking them out when they are lost, we find you.

The Christmas Flower

Readings: Zech 2:14-17 or Rev 11:19a; 12:1-6a, 10ab; Luke 1:26-38 or Luke 1:39-47

Scripture:
"And how does this happen to me,
that the mother of my Lord should come to me?
For at the moment the sound of your greeting reached my
    ears,
the infant in my womb leaped for joy." (Luke 1:43-44)

Reflection: Twelve days from now our church and homes will be decorated with the flower of Christmas: the poinsettia.

The poinsettia is an unlikely choice to become the "Christmas flower." It is found only in Central America and blooms just a few weeks in winter. The ancient Aztecs extracted a purplish dye from the plant for textiles and used its sap to treat fevers. The poinsettia would have remained a regional oddity were it not for Joel Roberts Poinsett, the first U.S. ambassador to Mexico in 1825. A physician and botanist, he sent some of the beautiful plants to his home in South Carolina and began growing them and giving them to friends and fellow botanists.

The Mexicans have a charming legend about the plant, in which a little girl was devastated because she was too poor to take any gifts to her church's nativity scene. An angel appeared to the despondent girl and told her to pick a weed, take it to the altar, and wait. The child did as the angel directed. When she placed the weed before the Christ Child, it had been transformed into a tall beautiful plant bearing a whorl of brilliant scarlet flowers on the top—the poinsettia.

From the ancient Aztec culture comes one of the most beautiful symbols of Christmas. Its medicinal properties reflect those of the healing Jesus; its deep red color reflects the cross he was born to embrace; its blooming in the middle of winter mirrors the love of God dawning in our sin and alienation; its legend exalts God's Spirit of generosity and compassion.

Like the poinsettia, today's feast of Our Lady of Guadalupe reminds us that Christmas is much larger than our provincial traditions and perspectives. Today we remember Mary's appearance to a people caught between two worlds: their ancient culture displaced by a new civilization from a land far away. Mary comes not as the European Madonna of their conquerors but as the mother in *mesitza* (Mexican) appearance and dress who adopts the subjected peasantry as her children. Our Lady of Guadalupe reveals a God whose compassion transcends labels and stereotypes, nationalities and races, creeds and class distinctions.

Meditation: Who do you know who would welcome the gift of a poinsettia plant this Christmas?

Prayer: Come, Lord, and make your dwelling among us. May we embrace the Guadalupe vision, recognizing you in the faces of our brothers and sisters. May we learn the parable of the poinsettia: that Christ comes to give his life so that we may be healed and brought to new life.

December 13: Thursday of the Second Week of Advent

Maiden of Light and Bread

Readings: Isa 41:13-20; Matt 11:11-15

Scripture:
"Amen, I say to you, among those born of women
there has been none greater than John the Baptist;
yet the least in the Kingdom of heaven is greater than he."
   (Matt 11:11)

Reflection: Today we remember and honor the maiden of light and bread.

December 13 is the feast of St. Lucy, a young woman—probably only in her teens—who was martyred in Sicily in the third century. The man she refused to marry denounced her as a Christian, and she was beheaded during the persecutions of Emperor Diocletian.

The name "Lucy" means "light." For centuries those suffering from blindness and diseases of the eye have sought help from St. Lucy, the patron saint of eyesight.

Sweden has a special devotion to St. Lucy. According to one legend, St. Lucy miraculously brought bread to feed Swedish children during a terrible famine. Lucy appeared, it is said, wearing a crown of light. And so began the custom that is still observed in many Swedish homes: on December 13, the eldest daughter of the family rises before dawn to prepare breads and pastries for the household. Then, dressed in a white robe and wearing a crown of candles, she serves her parents and brothers and sisters the breads she has prepared, as St. Lucy did centuries before.

In the old Julian calendar, the feast of St. Lucy was the shortest day of the year. Saint Lucy was the "light saint" who turned away the winter darkness on her feast day with the return of longer days. "St. Lucy fires" and "St. Lucy candles" were burned everywhere on December 13 to celebrate the sun's return.

The themes of this Advent season—light, joy, expectation—come together in the life of the young St. Lucy. By her death, she gives witness to the return of the risen Lord; the legends she has inspired mirror the risen One's light of love and compassion.

Meditation: What dark places of your life would you like to illuminate with the light of Christmas hope?

Prayer: God of light, Giver of our daily bread, may we become light and bread for others this Christmas. May the world see in us, as in your daughter Lucy, the Christ who comes to save us.

December 14: Friday of the Second Week of Advent

Discovering Life in Its Struggles

Readings: Isa 48:17-19; Matt 11:16-19

Scripture:
"To what shall I compare this generation?
It is like children who sit in marketplaces and call to one
    another,
'We played the flute for you, but you did not dance,
we sang a dirge but you did not mourn.'" (Matt 11:16-17)

Reflection: Walking in the woods one day, a boy finds the cocoon of a monarch butterfly. He watches the butterfly struggle to force its way through the tiny hole in the cocoon's casing. Then it seems to stop making progress: the butterfly seems to be stuck. Concerned that the butterfly is in trouble, the boy takes out a small knife he has in his pocket and carefully cuts away the rest of the cocoon. The butterfly emerges easily—but its body is swollen and small and its wings are all shriveled. The boy expects that at any moment the wings will begin to enlarge and expand and the butterfly will take flight.

But it never happens.

The boy does not understand that the butterfly's struggle through the restricted cocoon forces fluid from the body into the wings, giving the wings stability and strength so that the butterfly is ready to fly once it works its way through the cocoon. The young savior wannabe does not realize that the butterfly's freedom and flight are only possible because of the struggle and hardship it must undergo.

Like the kind but inexperienced boy who tries to help the struggling butterfly, we seek to avoid what is painful, stressful, and traumatic. We want to "fix" things; we want to save ourselves and those we love from hurt and struggle. But it is in failure that we learn; it is in suffering that we find healing; it is in our crosses that we discover the wholeness and joy of the resurrection.

The people of Jesus' time have dismissed John's hard admonitions to repentance and conversion; they have written off Jesus' teachings of "God's reign" centered in the human heart as simplistic and a disaster waiting to happen. But Jesus challenges them—and us—to realize the wisdom of John's call to reconciliation and forgiveness and his own gospel of love and compassion. If we are willing to see beyond ourselves, if we hear the many different voices in which God is speaking, God's wisdom will take root in us, re-creating and transforming our lives into that of God's.

Meditation: What gospel teaching of Jesus do you find most difficult to grasp? Despite your misgivings, how do you see those words of Jesus as a reality in your life?

Prayer: Lord Jesus, open our hearts and minds to accept what we find hard to understand, to see what is hidden from us, to hear what the noise and clamor of the world shout down. By your light, may we make our way to your holy mountain; by your grace, may we overcome the struggles and obstacles we encounter on our journey to your dwelling place.

December 15: Saturday of the Second Week of Advent

Elijah's Fiery Return

Readings: Sir 48:1-4, 9-11; Matt 17:9a, 10-13

Scripture:
"Elijah will indeed come and restore all things;
but I tell you that Elijah has already come." (Matt 17:11-12a)

Reflection: Elijah is the most revered prophet in Judaism. He appears about nine hundred years before Christ, dressed in the animal skins and leather belt common to his clan of shepherds, when God calls him to confront King Ahab and his consort Jezebel (1 Kgs 16–19).

Under Ahab and Jezebel, Israel has abandoned the worship of Yahweh and embraced the fertility cult of Baal. Elijah prophesies a three-year drought in Israel until the country returns to God. The drought ends with a contest between Elijah and the priests of Baal on Mount Carmel: whoever's "god" would answer his prophet's call with fire from heaven would be vindicated as the true divinity. Yahweh responds to Elijah's call with an awesome display of pyrotechnic power. The cult of Baal is destroyed.

The book of Kings recounts many other stories of Elijah's healings and prophecies. According to 2 Kings 2:1-11, Elijah did not die but was carried to heaven in a chariot of horses and fire. Rabbinic tradition says that Elijah will return to announce the coming of the Messiah. In Jewish homes at

Passover, a glass of wine is traditionally poured for Elijah, in expectation of his return. In the gospel accounts of Jesus' transfiguration, the two great figures of Jewish history appear with him on Mount Tabor: Moses the lawgiver and Elijah the prophet.

For Judaism, Elijah is the great prophet who will come and restore the world to peace and justice before the coming of the Messiah. For the people of the gospel, Elijah has returned in the person of John the Baptizer, who announces the coming of the Christ.

Our world is still in need of the fire of Elijah—the passionate commitment to restore the justice and mercy of God in our moment of history. As did the people who lined the Jordan River banks to hear John, we long to hear the same wonderful news: that God has come.

Meditation: How can you bring a measure of justice into your family or household this Christmas?

Prayer: Make us your prophets in our own time and place, O saving God. Ignite in us the fire of Elijah, that we may proclaim, in our commitment to ethics and morality, your reign of justice and reconciliation. Open our lips to speak the good news of John, that in our compassion and humility, we may proclaim your love in our midst.

THIRD WEEK OF ADVENT

December 16: Third Sunday of Advent

Your Christmas Gift List

Readings: Zeph 3:14-18a; Phil 4:4-7; Luke 3:10-18

Scripture:
[John] went throughout [the] whole region of the Jordan, proclaiming a baptism of repentance for the forgiveness of sins. (Luke 3:3)

Reflection: *What do you want for Christmas?*

Every December, the Santas in our lives ask what gifts we would like to find under the tree on Christmas morning. Then they go to work to make those wishes a reality.

What do you want for Christmas?

Now, the austere John the Baptizer (who will never be confused for jolly old St. Nick) asks us for a much more profound and urgent wish list. John asks this Advent, *What are you WANTING FOR this Christmas?* What emptiness do you ache to fill? What is missing from your life that God alone can complete?

From the River Jordan, John asks every one of us, of every time and place, *What do you HOPE FOR this Christmas?* What would make this Christmas whole, complete, new? A friendship restored? A relationship renewed? A chance to make things right?

And John challenges us with the most Christmas-like of questions: *What would you like to GIVE this Christmas?* What gifts do you hope to give that can't be wrapped and placed under the tree? Patience? Understanding? Reconciliation? What would you be willing to give up to make this Christmas special for someone else? Your expectation of restitution? Your obsession for control? Your need to be loved?

Consider what John asks: *What do you want this Christmas?*

The mystery of Christmas calls us to a much different approach to gift giving. Real Christmas gift giving reflects the God who empties himself of his divinity in order to remake humanity in his holiness; the gifts we give should mirror the love of this God, a love too complete and generous for us to imagine. The true gifts of Christmas that God gives us and enables us to give transform the hearts and lives of those we love: gifts of comfort and support, of compassion and reconciliation, of forgiveness and understanding.

Meditation: What one "gift" would you like to receive this Christmas that would bring fulfillment or healing to every season of your life?

Prayer: O God of compassion, you know our needs better than we do. Come, make your dwelling place in our hearts, illuminating our consciences with your wisdom, healing our brokenness with reconciliation, alleviating our fears with hope, filling our spirits with grace.

Christmas Cards and Family Photos

Readings: Gen 49:2, 8-10; Matt 1:1-17

Scripture:
The book of the genealogy of Jesus Christ,
the son of David, the son of Abraham. (Matt 1:1)

Reflection: At some point this holiday season, pour yourself a glass of Christmas cheer and get comfortable by the Christmas tree. Maybe play your favorite Christmas music. Then read the stack of Christmas cards you have received these past few weeks, reconnecting with those in the enclosed photographs. You'll experience a sense of gratitude and realize how blessed are the friendships that you have sustained since college, the friendships you've made in your parish and community, the friendships that have developed from shared experiences and memories.

During this season of making family memories, make it a point to sit down with your children and grandchildren and show them your family photographs. Tell them the stories of the great-grandfather who fought heroically during World War II, the grandmother who was such a marvelous cook, the artistic aunt and the skilled uncle, the cousin who inspired the entire family with a valiant fight against cancer. Those stories are your children's and grandchildren's stories as well.

Every moment of time is connected—one memory is the entry to another, one story sets the stage for the next. Today's gospel is a connection of such memories. While the historical accuracy of this list is dubious, Matthew's compilation points to Jesus as the fulfillment of a world that God envisioned from the first moment of creation. It is a vision that includes desert nomads and kings, shepherds and craftsmen, saints and sinners, men and women. It is a vision that transcends geography, culture, status—and even time itself.

And it is a vision that includes all of us—and our children and grandchildren and their children and grandchildren. As God called the generations from Abraham to Joseph and Mary of the first Advent to prepare for the appearance of Christ, God calls us in our own time, the days of the second Advent, to prepare for the reappearance of Christ in the fulfillment of time—to embrace the hope and potential of this life and to realize what an extraordinary gift is this life that God has breathed into us.

Meditation: In what ways do you feel "connected" to your parents' generation and your children and grandchildren? How do your best friendships make you aware of your connectedness to something greater than yourself?

Prayer: God of all times and seasons, you reveal your love in every generation; your presence blesses us in every loving, nurturing friendship. As we have experienced your generous and healing love within our families, may we be vessels of that love for those who follow us; may our friendships with others mirror our lasting and loving relationship with you, the Source of all that is good and loving.

The Risk of Being a Parent

Readings: Jer 23:5-8; Matt 1:18-25

Scripture:
"Joseph, Son of David,
do not be afraid to take Mary your wife into your home.
For it is through the Holy Spirit
that this child has been conceived in her." (Matt 1:20)

Reflection: Ann Hood and her husband lived a parent's worst nightmare: burying their child. At the age of five, their daughter died of a virulent form of strep. It was devastating.

Their family became "whole" again three years later when they traveled to China to adopt a little girl, Annabelle.

One morning, while everyone in the family was getting ready for school and work, Ann went into the bathroom and found Annabelle lying limp on the floor. Ann and Lance raced Annabelle to the hospital. They were reliving the same nightmare. This time, thankfully, Annabelle survived.

The experience left Ann shaken but with a new understanding of parenthood. She writes,

> A friend of mine whose father was murdered . . . told me that
> when her infant son's terminal illness was diagnosed, she told
> the doctor, "You must be mistaken. I've already had mine."
> Hadn't I already had mine? . . . What I do know is this: there
> is no safe route through parenthood, or even through life.
> When we offer our heart to others, we do not know what will

happen to it. It might break. It may grow. It might take us to places we never imagined. But isn't that the risk of love?

Matthew's story of Jesus' birth is the heartbreaking story of a young unmarried woman suddenly finding herself pregnant and her hurt and confused husband-to-be wondering what to do. In Matthew's gospel, Jesus' birth is a scandal—but in the midst of the embarrassment and confusion, God chooses to come into these broken lives, enabling Joseph and Mary to transform this messy situation through compassion, generosity, and trust into the dawning of Emmanuel.

Being a parent is risky and terrifying; it demands everything we have and are; it is filled with pain and doubt and despair. Yet to be a parent is to be a coworker with the Father of all, God the Parent whose love for his sons and daughters knows neither limit nor condition. In the struggles of fear and anguish experienced by the Holy Family, we realize that the light of God shines in the midst of our own families as we confront those same tensions and crises in our life together.

Meditation: How have you experienced the "risk" of loving another, whether a spouse, child, or friend?

Prayer: O God, may we be inspired by the selfless compassion and unwavering devotion of Joseph and Mary so that we may be "Josephs" and "Marys" to our families. In times of crisis and tension, bless our families with the hope of your consolation; in times of joy and discovery, bless us with a spirit of gratitude, and never let us forget that you are the Father of us all, the Giver of all that is good.

December 19: Wednesday in Late Advent

Listening to the "Voices"

Readings: Judg 13:2-7, 24-25a; Luke 1:5-25

Scripture:
[T]he angel of the Lord appeared to [Zechariah],
standing at the right of the altar of incense. . . .
"Do not be afraid, Zechariah,
because your prayer has been heard.
Your wife Elizabeth will bear you a son,
and you shall name him John." (Luke 1:11, 13)

Reflection: In George Bernard Shaw's play *Saint Joan*, Joan, the uneducated but determined farm girl, wears down the dauphin, France's ruler in exile, with her claims that the voices she has heard have sent her to restore the young ruler to the throne of France. At one point, the exasperated dauphin cries, "Oh, your voices, your voices! Why don't the voices come to me? I am king, not you!"

Joan replies, "They do come to you but you do not hear them. You have not sat in the evening listening to them. When the angelus [bell] rings you cross yourself and [you are] done with it; but if you prayed from your heart and listened to the trilling of the bells in the air after they stopped ringing, you would hear the voices as well as I do."

In many of the gospels of Advent, the "voice" of God speaks to individuals in dreams and through the appearance of angels.

Today we hear the story of Zechariah's vision, his hearing the "voice" of God as he went about his duties as a priest in the temple. But the poor man is overwhelmed: all too aware of his weaknesses and doubts and the reality of his age and position, he cannot grasp the "good news" that God is calling him to embrace. But in God's good time, Zechariah comes to understand and accept the wonderful possibilities God lays before him and his beloved Elizabeth.

The voice of God speaks to each one of us as well, in the silence of our hearts, in the compassion of others, in the cries of the hurting and desperate. What is required of us, as the young Joan understands, is an open heart to listen and to imagine the possibilities for God's light to illuminate our lives and transform our spirits.

Meditation: What do you hear God saying to you in the depths of your heart?

Prayer: Open our hearts this Advent, O God, to hear your voice speaking to us constantly and insistently in the sacred silence of our hearts. Give us the courage to follow your "voice" so that we may dare to hope in the fulfillment of your Easter promise in the Advent of our lives.

Everyday "Annunciations"

Readings: Isa 7:10-14; Luke 1:26-38

Scripture:
[T]he angel Gabriel was sent from God
to a town of Galilee called Nazareth,
to a virgin betrothed to a man named Joseph,
of the house of David,
and the virgin's name was Mary. (Luke 1:26-27)

Reflection: She had not talked to her friend for some time and wondered how she was doing. She had heard that the family was going through a tough time. One morning, she saw that a movie they both were looking forward to seeing had opened. So she called her: "Hi. Would you like to take in a movie this afternoon?" After a pause, her friend said, "You know, that would be great. It would give us a chance to talk." *Hail, full of grace! The Lord is with you. Blessed are you.*

The chair of the college's education department asked her to come in. "A downtown church is organizing an after-school program for at-risk kids," he explained. "They've asked if any of our students could serve as tutors. You have a real gift for working with children and you're going to make a great teacher. So I thought of you immediately." She wondered how she could work it into her busy class schedule; and she didn't have anywhere near the confidence in herself that her professor clearly had. But, in the end, she said, "I'd like to try." *The Holy Spirit will come upon you and the power of God will overshadow you. Nothing is impossible for God.*

After her father's death from Alzheimer's disease, she began making an annual gift to the Alzheimer's Association. One day she received a call asking if she would help organize a "memory walk" for Alzheimer's research. As she talked to the volunteer, her eyes fell on a photo of her dad on her desk. "Yes, I'd love to help." *I am the handmaid of the Lord. May it be done.*

It may seem that annunciations only happen to Mary and figures in the Bible—but the fact is that God calls every one of us to the vocation of prophet, the ministry of charity, the work of reconciliation. Gabriel may come in the form of an invitation, a plea, a concern for another's well-being. Like Mary, we think of all kinds of reasons why this doesn't make any sense or that this task is beyond us, but it is in these everyday annunciations that God changes the course of history. In the Advents of our lives, God calls us to bring his Christ into our time and place; may we respond with the faith and trust of Mary, putting aside our doubts and fears to say, *I am your servant, O God. Be it done.*

Meditation: Have you ever realized God calling you in the midst of the everyday and ordinary?

Prayer: O Lord, our Father and Redeemer, may we realize the many ways you "announce" to us your presence in our midst and your invitation to reveal that presence to others. Instill in us the generosity of heart and perseverance of spirit to let your call to your work of compassion and reconciliation "be done" in our homes and hearts.

Elizabeth and Zechariah

Readings: Song 2:8-14 or Zeph 3:14-18a; Luke 1:39-45

Scripture:
Elizabeth, filled with the Holy Spirit,
cried out in a loud voice and said,
"Most blessed are you among women,
and blessed is the fruit of your womb." (Luke 1:41-42)

Reflection: Gabriel, before his visit to Mary with news of her motherhood, appears to Zechariah as he was performing his priestly duties in the sanctuary of the temple. Gabriel tells him that God will give him a son who will be the last great prophet of the coming of the Messiah.

His wife, Elizabeth, greets the news with unbounded joy. Her greeting to Mary reflects her gratitude. Elizabeth possesses the depth of spirit to see God's hand in all of this—and the courage and trust to welcome it. Her ability to recognize the holy in her midst enables her to welcome and support Mary in her young cousin's most traumatic hour; it gives her the strength to bear the physical pain of bearing a child at her own advanced age.

For Zechariah, however, this makes no sense. Ironically, he, the "professional religious" in the family, cannot see the hand of God. While he is a man of faithfulness and goodness, he also possesses the cynicism that comes with age. His understanding is limited by human considerations: *We're too old for this to happen.* Gabriel makes Zechariah speechless until "the days these things take place."

When their son is born, Zechariah is asked for his name. Zechariah writes on a tablet, "John is his name." Zechariah now understands what God has called them to do and accepts that role. Zechariah's speech is a beautiful canticle praising God's goodness and prophesying the wonderful things that his son John will accomplish.

Our own struggle with faith is reflected in the story of Elizabeth and Zechariah. Sometimes the disappointments we have experienced make us unable to perceive God in our midst; the overwhelming demands of career and family shut out God's call to us to be bearers of his life and love. Whether we respond to God with the immediate joy of Elizabeth or we struggle like Zechariah to make sense of it all, God continues with us and for us; God's love remains in our midst until we are ready to embrace it.

Meditation: When was the last time you reacted to circumstances with the doubt of Zechariah but eventually coped with the situation with the optimism of Elizabeth?

Prayer: God of all times and ages, come and make your dwelling place in our midst. May we welcome you with joy and faith, that the world may not harden our hearts and the disappointments we experience in this life not jade us from beholding your presence in the love around us.

December 22: Saturday in Late Advent

The Gospel's First Preacher

Readings: 1 Sam 1:24-28; Luke 1:46-56

Scripture:
"My soul proclaims the greatness of the Lord;
my spirit rejoices in God my savior." (Luke 1:46-47)

Reflection: The image we have of Mary is usually that of one of her statues or paintings: the flawless representations of her in the Christmas manger, the exquisite vision seen at Fatima and Lourdes, the otherworldly iconography of her holding the Child-God-King.

She is beautiful and holy—and remote.

But the Mary of the gospels is a real woman who pays a heavy price for her "yes" to God: a painful confrontation with her beloved Joseph when her pregnancy is revealed; a dangerous trip to Bethlehem; the excruciating pain of giving birth, alone, in a barn; the desperate escape to Egypt; the helplessness of watching her innocent son's death. Mary is not the quiet, diffident bystander as she is often pictured in iconography but a real woman who knows all the joys and struggles of parenthood, poverty, and life at its messiest.

In today's gospel, Luke portrays Mary in a role we would never imagine for her—for Luke, Mary is the first preacher of the gospel. The words she says to Elizabeth—the canticle we know as the *Magnificat*—is the first proclamation of the gospel. It is anything but the pious ode of a plastic saint: it is a prophetic, cutting-edge declaration of faith and trust in the living, creative presence of God.

Mary understands what God will do in the child she will bear. She knows that in the promise she has received from God, history is about to be turned upside down. Furthermore, she realizes that she herself is the first instance of this new upside-down world: she is the small one whom God has lifted up; she is the lowly servant on whom God has looked with favor.

Mary embodies the good news she proclaims: the gospel of forgiveness, humble service to others, justice, and, ultimately, resurrection.

Meditation: What one line or image from Mary's *Magnificat* strikes you as especially prophetic and inspiring?

Prayer: Father, as Mary welcomed your Christ, may we welcome your Word of compassion and peace into our midst; as she journeyed with her son to Jerusalem, may we journey with him and take up our crosses; as she held the broken body of her son, may we hold and support and heal one another in our brokenness and pain; as she realized the promise of her son's resurrection, may we realize that promise in our lives as well. May Mary's arms become our arms; may her journey become our journey; may her song of faith and hope become our song.

FOURTH WEEK OF ADVENT

Visitations

Readings: Mic 5:1-4a; Heb 10:5-10; Luke 1:39-45

Scripture:
"Blessed are you among women,
and blessed is the fruit of your womb." (Luke 1:42)

Reflection: Every Monday morning for sixteen weeks they leave their house at dawn for their eight a.m. appointment at the hospital. For the four hours that her twelve-year-old daughter undergoes chemotherapy, Mom will be right there. During the treatments, they will read, play games, watch videos, talk. Their Monday mornings are anxious times, but precious. For this mother and daughter, the Spirit of Mary's Child is with them.

Every Tuesday afternoon, after a full day of her own classes, Kristen, a high school senior, heads to the community center. For two hours, she tutors kids from city grammar schools in the mysteries of math and the secrets of English grammar and vocabulary. In Kristen's patient explanations and words of encouragement, God's compassion is revealed to kids at risk.

It is the first time the brothers have spoken in years. They've been estranged over a family matter, the details of which are long forgotten but the hurt and mistrust have lingered. But for the good of the family, they seek to repair their broken relationship. In every awkward word exchanged, in every attempt to move on, in every admission of hurt and anger between the two brothers, God is reborn.

In today's gospel, Mary travels "in haste" to be with her cousin Elizabeth. Luke never says exactly why she goes, but we can guess: Mary wants to be with her beloved cousin in the last months of what must have been a very difficult pregnancy, but also to seek the elder Elizabeth's counsel and support during her own struggle to understand what is happening. In Mary and Elizabeth's time together and in our own similar "visitations," the Spirit of God is present in the healing, comfort, and support we can extend to one another in such moments. In the stirring of the infant in Elizabeth's womb, God calls to humanity in every time and place: *I am with you every step of the way. I am with you in every storm. I am with you when the night seems unending.* In Mary's Child, the inexplicable love of God becomes real to us; the peace and justice of God become possible.

Meditation: When have you experienced within your own family relationships the loving presence of God?

Prayer: Come, Lord, and make your place in the midst of our families and households. By your grace, may we, like Mary, "make haste" to be with one another in times of crisis, hurt, and estrangement; like Elizabeth, may we be sources of understanding and compassion for the members of our families.

December 24: Monday of Late Advent (Christmas Eve)

"Let Every Heart Prepare Him Room"

Readings: 2 Sam 7:1-5, 8b-12, 14a, 16; Luke 1:67-79

Scripture:
"In the tender compassion of our God
the dawn from on high shall break upon us,
to shine on those who dwell in darkness and the shadow
  of death,
and to guide our feet into the way of peace." (Luke 1:78-79)

Reflection: He is never mentioned in Luke's story of Jesus' birth in Bethlehem, but he is the linchpin of the whole Christmas story. Were it not for him, Jesus would not have been born in a poor stable but in the Bethlehem Ramada.

He is the innkeeper who presumably refused a room to Joseph and Mary, forcing them to find shelter in a barn. All Luke says is that "there was no room for them in the inn." But every Christmas pageant includes the innkeeper, often portrayed as a gruff old bird who cannot be bothered with a poor carpenter from the sticks and his young bride. Sometimes he is the harried host, overcome with the demands of running a hotel during the busy season. And once in a while, the innkeeper is a compassionate soul who sympathizes with these poor travelers and offers the only hospitality he can.

The innkeeper never realizes who he is turning away. It is a busy time: guests and customers need to be taken care of, and the place is filling up faster than he and his wife can keep up with. *Nothing personal, folks—it's the busy season.*

We should not be too quick to ridicule: we're all innkeepers when it comes to this Child. Things need to be taken care of, our lives fill up faster than we can cope. *Nothing personal, Jesus.*

The innkeeper's plight is the challenge of Christmas: to make room in our homes and hearts for this Child, in the midst of the demanding commerce of our professions and careers, in the quiet desperation of our pain and anguish, at our kitchen table and in our classrooms, in our wallets and checkbooks, in our calendars and day planners; to make room for him both when he is welcome and when his presence is embarrassing and inconvenient.

This will probably be a busy day as you get ready for tomorrow. But take a moment in the midst of the day's preparations to remember that Christ comes in every guest who comes to your inn. In every season of the New Year, make a place for the Child in the Bethlehem of your heart in every season of the New Year.

Meditation: How can your experience of hospitality—either as a host or guest—mirror that of the Child of Bethlehem?

Prayer: In the birth of your Son, O God, you have touched human history. May the dawning of Christ illuminate every morning; may his birth re-create every human heart; may his presence among us transform our stables and inns into holy places of your compassion and peace.

SEASON OF CHRISTMAS

December 25: The Nativity of the Lord (Christmas)

"Unto Certain Shepherds"

Readings:
VIGIL: Isa 62:1-5; Acts 13:16-17, 22-25; Matt 1:1-25
  (or 1:18-25)
MIDNIGHT: Isa 9:1-6; Titus 2:11-14; Luke 2:1-14
DAWN: Isa 62:11-12; Titus 3:4-7; Luke 2:15-20
DAY: Isa 52:7-10; Heb 1:1-6; John 1:1-18 (or 1:1-5, 9-14)

Scripture:
Now there were shepherds in that region living in the fields
and keeping the night watch over their flock.
The angel of the Lord appeared to them
and the glory of the Lord shone around them,
and they were struck with great fear. (Luke 2:8-9)

Reflection: The shepherds of Luke's gospel are the blank page in the Christmas story. Luke says nothing of how many there were, where they came from, or where they went.

Yet they are first to hear the "good news for all the people."

Shepherds were not the idyllic pastoral figures we imagine, as peaceful and gentle as the lambs they tended. In reality, shepherds were tough, earthy characters, who fearlessly swung their clubs against poachers and wild animals. It was not a job for the faint of heart or affable of disposition: they confronted the most ruthless thieves, the wildest animals, and the worst weather. The pompous Pharisees and scribes regarded shepherds as a disreputable and untrustworthy lot of rustics; they were considered second-class citizens and were barred from Jewish courts of law and synagogues.

Simple shepherds rather than the world's powerful and elite are the first to behold the birth of humanity's Savior—the Christ who would portray himself as the "Good Shepherd" whose love and compassion for humanity would know neither end nor limitation. The shepherds are everyone of everyday life—albeit at life's harder edges. Throughout his gospel narrative, Luke points to the faithful poor, the desperate souls who continue to hope in God's goodness, who recognize and welcome the Christ in their midst.

May we possess the simple hearts of the Bethlehem shepherds to hear and embrace the good news of Jesus' birth; may we possess that spirit of humility that enables us to rejoice in the wondrous love of our God revealed this night.

Meditation: How does God reveal his presence in the simplest, everyday moments of your life?

Prayer: Lord God, may we behold the joy of your birth with the humble gratitude of the shepherds. May the grace of your Christ who comes to shepherd us help us to care for one another; may the good news we hear in our struggling Bethlehems bring joy and hope to all our mornings; may your coming to us as one of us inspire us to lift up one another in the dignity of being your sons and daughters.

December 26: Saint Stephen, First Martyr

Of Gods and Men

Readings: Acts 6:8-10; 7:54-59; Matt 10:17-22

Scripture:
As they were stoning Stephen, he called out
"Lord Jesus, receive my spirit." (Acts 7:59)

Reflection: The extraordinary French film *Of Gods and Men* recounts the true story of a small monastery of Trappist monks in a mountain village of Algeria in the 1990s. In the gruesome violence of the Algerian civil war, the community of eight monks was an oasis of peace and compassion in the midst of the horror around them. The monks lived humbly and happily among their Muslim neighbors in the village of Tibhirine, keeping their garden and bees, offering hospitality in their guesthouse and medical care to all who came to their small clinic. They did not try to convert any of their Muslim neighbors to Catholicism; the simple generosity of their lives was a bridge between Christianity and Islam.

As the violence escalated, the government urged the monks to abandon the abbey. The monks anguished over what to do.

A Muslim villager asked one of the monks if they were going to leave. A brother shrugged, "We're like birds on a branch. We don't know if we'll leave."

But a woman of the village pleaded, "No, we are the birds. You are the branch. If you go, we'll lose our footing."

From the days of Stephen, martyrs throughout the centuries have given their lives for the sake of gospel compassion and justice. Even in our own time, men and women like the monks of Tibhirine give their lives in witness to the gospel of reconciliation and justice. They realize that the gift of faith requires us to become "branches" of God's justice, compassion, and forgiveness; that real faith is to understand, in the clarity of God's love, how blessed we have been and to see ourselves and others as brother and sister "servants" at the table of the Father. The brothers accept the reality that the gospel that begins in a Bethlehem stable continues on to the tree of the cross on a hillside outside of Jerusalem, but they carry on in the joy and assurance that their crucifixions and stonings will be vehicles of Easter resurrection.

Meditation: Who in your life is a "branch" of stability and wisdom for you in your struggle to live Jesus' gospel?

Prayer: God of compassion, fill us with your spirit as you filled your son Stephen; make us "branches" of reconciliation and peace as were the Trappists at Tibhirine. By your grace, may we imitate the courage of Stephen and the brothers to be prophets of your justice despite the risk of rejection and ridicule; by your spirit, help us to become, like them, disciples of your Son's compassion in our time and place.

December 27: Saint John, Apostle and Evangelist

The Help

Readings: 1 John 1:1-4; John 20:1a, 2-8

Scripture:
They both ran, but the other disciple ran faster than Peter
and arrived at the tomb first;
he bent down and saw the burial cloths there. . . .
[H]e saw and believed. (John 20:4–5, 8b)

Reflection: In Kathryn Stockett's wonderful novel *The Help*
(on which the 2011 film is based), Skeeter Phelan, a would-be
writer, returns to her hometown of Jackson, Mississippi, after
graduating from college in the early 1960s. Taking a job as the
household-tips columnist for the local newspaper, Skeeter
turns to Aibileen, a black maid who works for a friend's
family, for help in answering readers' questions about clean-
ing and cooking. In their unlikely friendship, Skeeter begins
to realize the quiet dignity of Aibileen and the unappreciated
black women who have spent their entire lives caring for the
children of their indifferent white employers. Skeeter urges
Aibileen and her friends to tell their stories for a book she
proposes to a New York publisher. Though written secretly
and published anonymously, the book is a dangerous under-
taking that puts them all at risk. But these noble black women
summon the courage to tell their stories.

Confronting the injustice of their lives and those of their families and the light they can bring to the darkness of racism, the sisterhood of Jackson's black maids recount their stories in the same spirit and with the same urgency that the evangelist John (whose feast we celebrate today) chronicles his story of Jesus.

The story of *The Help* is a story of re-creation, of hope, of resurrection. Their stories and stories like theirs remind us that Easter is more than an event: Easter is an attitude, a perspective, a light to guide us along this path of stones we stumble along; Easter is the love that pulls us out of our tombs of fear and hopelessness. Easter is to realize that we are embraced by God in the embrace of one another.

At Christmas we discover new hope; we "behold" new possibilities for justice, for peace, for forgiveness in our Advent lives. In our baptism into his life, Christ calls us to tell the story we have heard and help others realize that Easter promise in their lives.

Meditation: In what ways can you tell the "story" of the risen Jesus in your everyday life?

Prayer: O God, in your compassion and peace you have brought resurrection to our Advent lives. May we now become tellers of that story in the compassion we extend and receive, in the gospel principles of justice and forgiveness we practice, in our efforts to "make flesh" your Word of reconciliation and peace.

December 28: Feast of the Holy Innocents, Martyrs

The Innocent Among Us

Readings: 1 John 1:5–2:2; Matt 2:13-18

Scripture:
When Herod realized that he had been deceived by the
  magi,
he became furious.
He ordered the massacre of all the boys in Bethlehem and
  its vicinity
two years old and under,
in accordance with the time he had ascertained from the
  magi. (Matt 2:16)

Reflection: A little girl walking home from school is hit by
a car driven by a man who has had too much to drink.

A young mother, whose husband walked out, struggles
to raise her three children on her waitressing pay and tips.

Jobless parents become more and more desperate as their
unemployment benefits end—with no employment prospects in sight.

A terrified family huddles in the basement as the winds
and rains batter their small house; thousands of miles away,
another family stands helplessly in what is left of their small
garden plot that drought has ravaged to dust.

A young man lies in bed, hooked up to a variety of tubes
and monitors, trying to remain hopeful in the face of the
inevitable.

They are the innocent victims of the irresponsibility and selfishness of others, of devastating natural disasters and catastrophic illness. Every time and every place have known the suffering innocent—often forgotten, often ignored, often overlooked.

Today's gospel recounts the innocent children who are murdered by Herod in his obsessive rage to destroy the Christ. The feast of the Holy Innocents reminds us that God dies in the death of every innocent who is destroyed by the self-absorbed and greedy Herods of history's Palestines; God cries out in the lamentations of every Rachel who mourns for her innocent sons and daughters. In Christ, God calls us to the work of transforming the suffering and death of the innocent into God's rule of justice and peace.

Meditation: Who are the innocent you know who are the victims of catastrophe and injustice not of their making? What can you do to alleviate their suffering?

Prayer: God of mercy, open our hearts to hear the cries of the many innocent victims of injustice, poverty, and prejudice. By your grace and their inspiration, may we work to bring comfort and healing, justice and freedom to a world broken and enslaved by avarice and ignorance.

Hopes and Dreams

Readings: 1 John 2:3-11; Luke 2:22-35

Scripture:
Simeon blessed them and said to Mary, his mother,
"Behold, this child is destined
for the rise and fall of many in Israel,
and to be a sign that will be contradicted
(and you yourself a sword will pierce)
so that the thoughts of many hearts may be revealed."
  (Luke 2:34-35)

Reflection: Two grandmothers were doing what grandmothers do when they get together: talk about their grandchildren. One grandmother was proudly showing off the latest photographs of her two grandchildren.

"Oh, they're so cute!" cooed her friend. "How old are they now?"

Pointing to each child in one of the photographs, the beaming grandmother said, "The lawyer is two and the doctor is four."

We all have such hopes and dreams for our children; we all know too well that life can be cruel to dreams and shatter many hopes, and we want to protect our sons and daughters from such realities. We want the best for our children—and we're willing to move any mountain and slay any dragon for them. Joseph and Mary confront those same hopes and fears in today's gospel. Every parent's life is "pieced" with turmoil, disappointment, illness, desperation, and fear. Certainly every mom and dad knows what Mary and Joseph went through.

Of course, hopes are revisited as expectations change; dreams are reimagined, as potential and possibility become clearer and more defined. But the most precious thing we can give our children is our faith in God's complete and unconditional love. We want our sons and daughters to embrace and be embraced by the love we have known and seek to know better; we want them to be grasped by the hand of God who has grasped us by the hand. It is as a family that children can best experience that love in their lives.

Oh, we dream all kinds of dreams for our children—from their becoming president to winning the Super Bowl. But the most important dream we can dream for them, the most important gift we can give them, is this: faith in the God who made them, faith in the God who loves them, faith in the God who will be with them on their road—wherever that road passes—to eternity.

Meditation: How can you be supportive of the dreams and hopes of members of your family?

Prayer: Father in heaven, we lift up our prayers to you for our children and all young people you have entrusted to us. By your healing grace, may we deal with the "swords" and contradictions that befall us. By the light of your wisdom, may we realize that our hopes are fulfilled in embracing and being embraced by your compassion.

December 30:
Feast of the Holy Family (Catholic Church)
Sunday after Christmas (Episcopal Church)

Lost in the Temple, Fleeing to Egypt

Readings: 1 Sam 1:20-22, 24-28; Col 3:12-21 (or 3:12-17) or
1 John 3:1-2, 21-24; Luke 2:41-52

Scripture:
After three days they found him in the temple,
sitting in the midst of the teachers,
listening to them and asking them questions. (Luke 2:46)

Reflection: All parents experience moments of sheer terror:
when their son wanders away at the mall, when their daughter comes down with an illness they have no idea how to
deal with. Along the way, they wonder how they are going
to pay the mortgage, the back-to-school clothes, the braces,
college tuition. There are many sleepless nights as their kids
cope with the new freedoms and responsibilities of adulthood. They second-guess their decisions on discipline, the
values they have tried to instill in their children, the advice
they have offered. Every moment of every day, moms and
dads ask why and how they can raise children when they
still feel like kids themselves. And those doubts and fears
continue when their children become parents.

Every family, at some time, has searched the temple for
the lost child, fled to Egypt in time of danger, faced scandal
and embarrassment together.

Mary, Joseph, and the Child's struggle as a family was filled with heartache, fear, misunderstanding, and doubt, but together they created a family of love and compassion, nurture and acceptance, trust and support. Within our own families, the love of God upholds us through life in all its disappointments and complexities. Today's feast is a celebration of family—that unique nucleus of society that gives life, nurture, and support throughout our journey. Families are the first and best places for the love of God to come alive.

Meditation: What has been the hardest situation your family has had to deal with? How were you able to cope with it?

Prayer: Heavenly Father, you have brought us together as a family and called us to the vocation of parenthood. Embrace our family in your loving providence. May your spirit of wisdom guide us as we raise and guide our children. In times of crisis and tension, bless our families with the hope of your consolation and forgiveness; in times of joy and growth, instill in us a spirit of thankfulness, never letting us forget that you are Father of us all.

God's Arms

Readings: 1 John 2:18-21; John 1:1-18

Scripture:
And the Word became flesh
and made his dwelling among us. (John 1:14)

Reflection: The English Protestant preacher Leslie Weather-head once told of a pastor who stopped by the home of a young woman whose husband had been buried the day before. They had only been married three months when a deadly form of pneumonia unexpectedly took the young man's life.

In the front room of the small house, an old white-haired woman sat in a low chair, her tired face half hidden by her hand; her other hand softly rubbed the shoulder of the young widow—little more than a girl—sitting at her feet.

Suddenly the woman turned almost ferociously on the pastor.

"Where is God?" she demanded. "I've prayed to Him. Where is He? You preached once on the 'Everlasting Arms of God.' Where are they?"

The minister drew his fingertips lightly down the older woman's arm.

"They are here," he said. "They are round you even now. These are the arms of God."

Christmas celebrates more than a single event, more than just the birth of a child in a Bethlehem cave long ago: Christmas celebrates a presence that continues to this day and for all time. That presence is experienced in every moment of compassion we extend and experience, every moment of comfort and consolation we offer and receive, every moment of forgiveness we seek and give.

"Emmanuel"—"God is with us." In Christ's birth, God touches human history: hope reigns, justice takes root, peace becomes possible. The challenge to each one of us is to take on the work of "Emmanuel"—to make God's presence tangible by being his arms for the hurting, his hands for the fallen, his heart for the grieving.

Meditation: When have you experienced the embrace of God in the concern and care of another—and when have you been God's "arms" for someone you love?

Prayer: Come, Lord, make your dwelling place in our midst. In the loving embrace of spouses and family, may we be embraced in your love; in the helping hand we extend to others and others extend to us, may we know the help of your wisdom and grace; in the comfort and consolation that heal us and that enable us to heal others, may we be healed by your reconciling peace.

January 1:
Solemnity of Mary, Mother of God (Catholic Church)
Holy Name of Jesus (Episcopal Church)

The Journal

Readings: Num 6:22-27; Gal 4:4-7; Luke 2:16-21

Scripture:
And Mary kept all these things,
reflecting on them in her heart. (Luke 2:19)

Reflection: They were celebrating their first New Year's together. Married that summer, they were caught up with typical first-year struggles: creating a home, balancing careers and marriage, keeping up with student and car loans while putting away whatever they could to build a future.

That New Year's Eve, they decided to stay home. He walked into the bedroom and found her writing in a notebook. Snuggling next to her, he asked what she was doing.

"Oh, nothing. Just writing all that's happened this year."

"Can I see?" he asked.

"Sure."

He started to read: *A beautiful wedding with family and friends . . . our honeymoon in Bermuda . . . Mom and Dad's help to buy our first place . . . my wonderful husband . . .*

Then he took the pen and added, *My brothers' help in fixing up our house . . . A tough but good year at the firm that shows promise . . . my loving, caring wife.*

"A pretty good first year," he said, handing back the pen.

She wrote at the end, *We have much to be grateful for.*

And so began a tradition. Every New Year's, they would open the notebook and list the blessings of the year past. In those early years, the list was long: *the birth of Sarah, her promotion, the launch of his own business.* Some years the list was short and almost terse: *Managed to keep it together during a bad year. Survived her cancer surgery. A stormy year with our teenager Sam, but we all made it.*

And every page ends, *We have much to be grateful for.*

Their journal now runs fifty-plus pages. Recent entries include the blessings of grandchildren; pasted inside are prayer cards remembering loved ones who have died.

The journal is kept on the top of a dresser where they can't help but see it every day. Its very presence throughout the year reminds them, *We have much to be grateful for.*

We are loved by a God who humbles himself to become one of us. In the love of this God we have much to be grateful for; in the complexities and challenges of our lives we realize that the truth of God's love is the one constant reality. May we find fulfillment and purpose, consolation and grace in our own gratefulness journals, in our mindfulness of the truth of the God of blessing and compassion.

Meditation: What would you write on this year's page of your own "gratefulness journal"?

Prayer: We thank you, O God, for the gift of the New Year. Inspired by your wisdom and grace, may we make the pages of 2013 a chronicle of your grace and peace in our midst.

January 2

Prophetess of Bread

Readings: 1 John 2:22-28; John 1:19-28

Scripture:
John answered them,
   "I baptize with water;
   but there is one among you whom you do not recognize,
   the one who is coming after me,
   whose sandal strap I am not worthy to untie."
      (John 1:26-27)

Reflection: British writer Margaret Silf recounts this story in an essay in *America* (July 6–13, 2009):

During World War II, a battered contingent of captured allied soldiers was marched through a German village. The streets were lined with onlookers, some smiling smugly, others wiping away tears of compassion for the plight of these poor soldiers, many of them boys. The starving prisoners were utterly exhausted, their eyes dark with despair.

The silence of the scene was broken when a woman broke through the crowd. The woman, a housewife and mother from the village, thrust a loaf of bread into one of the prisoner's hands before disappearing to her kitchen. Her risky act of compassion was soon taken up by others, who brought out food for the captives.

One woman's prophetic act of courageous generosity resulted in the transformation of enemy soldiers into sons and brothers.

To act "prophetically" begins with embracing what is right and just and then being willing to confront whatever evil seeks to destroy that good. In baptism, all of us are called to be prophets of God's goodness and justice, however unpopular that prophetic act may make us, whatever cost such prophesy exacts from us.

In response to the priests and Levites who have come to meet him, John says humbly that he baptizes "with water" in anticipation of the Christ who comes. We too can give voice to the coming of the Christ in the simple "water" we have at our disposal: the water of understanding, the water of comfort, the water of charity. Our sharing the "water" of peace with others and our breaking of the "bread" of compassion with those in need are prophetic acts in which we create an entryway for God to enter our lives.

Meditation: When have you most recently experienced an act of kindness or generosity that you consider a "prophetic" act?

Prayer: O Lord, with the help of your grace to act prophetically with compassion and forgiveness, may we discern your will in the example of the prophets in our midst; may we possess the prophet's courage to "proclaim" your love in the love and compassion we give and receive.

January 3

God of Haute Cuisine, High Fashion, and Financial Portfolios

Readings: 1 John 2:29–3:6; John 1:29-34

Scripture:
"[T]he reason why I came baptizing with water
was that he might be made known to Israel." (John 1:31)

Reflection: He is the head chef at a very popular downtown restaurant. He loves his work, but he has discovered a passion for devising new recipes for the simple soups and entrees prepared by the dedicated volunteers at a nearby soup kitchen for their ever-increasing number of guests.

They are studying fashion design at an art institute. On their way to becoming the next Donna Karan or Tommy Hilfiger, they are presented with a challenge from a local social service agency: Could they design a lightweight, warm, waterproof coat that could be made inexpensively for the homeless—and could it have deep pockets and a lining that can be zipped out and used as a blanket or rain poncho? They spend weeks playing with designs and experimenting with fabrics—and talking with the homeless about their struggles and experiences. Finally, the student designers come up with a workable, practical design. With a grant from a church group, several coats are made and distributed. In their hearts, these students know, regardless of how successful they are in their careers, they will never make a more beautiful garment.

He manages portfolios worth millions of dollars. He knows how to make his clients' money work for them. But this smart, successful money manager is convinced that his most important work takes place on Tuesday evenings when he donates his time and expertise to offer free counseling to people living on the economic edge, to families in financial crisis, and to new start-ups in the inner city.

In the "water" from our baptisms, we continue what John began with the water of his baptizing at the Jordan: to make known Christ in our midst. With the "water" of generosity, of sacrifice, of compassion, we reveal the Lamb of God present in our time and place; we become vehicles for the Spirit of God to transform our broken world into the kingdom of God. Our "baptismal water" may take the form of a skillet or sewing machine, an ability to manage or design. In employing our talents in service to others, we reveal God's presence to those working hard to build meaningful lives for their families; using our treasure, we reveal God's compassion for those struggling to survive; from the lessons we have learned from pain and despair, we reveal God's hope to the despairing and desperate.

Meditation: In what "water" do you have that reveals God in our midst?

Prayer: Christ Jesus, the Lamb of God, may we behold your presence in our midst in every moment of the New Year. May your Spirit transform our perspective and actions so that we may bring to reality your reign of righteousness and reconciliation in our time and place.

"Let Jesus Show"

Readings: 1 John 3:7-10; John 1:35-42

Scripture:
John was standing with two of his disciples,
and as he watched Jesus walk by, he said,
"Behold, the Lamb of God." (John 1:35-36)

Reflection: In *Secrets in the Dark: A Life in Sermons*, writer and preacher Frederick Buechner tells the story of a nativity pageant staged by the children of the church. The manger was located in front of the altar steps. All the characters were there: Mary in blue mantle, Joseph in a cotton beard, three wise men, and a company of shepherds—with the baby Jesus lying in straw in the center of the scene. The nativity story was read by the pastor with carols sung at the appropriate places.

Everything was going according to the script until the arrival of the angels. The "heavenly host," all dressed in white, were scattered throughout the church, seated with their parents. On cue, the little angels were supposed to come forward and gather around the manger, singing, *Glory to God in the highest, and on earth peace, good will among men.* But because there were so many of them, the angels started to push and jockey for a place in the chancel. One angel, a girl about nine years old who was smaller than most of them, ended up so far out on the fringe of things that, even craning her neck and standing on tiptoes, she could not see. *Glory to God in the highest, and on earth peace, good will among men*, the company sang, and then, in the momentary pause that followed, the small girl electrified the entire church by crying out in a voice shrill with irritation and frustration and enormous sadness at having her view blocked, "Let Jesus show!"

The wise pastor decided to end the pageant right there, with a quick prayer and blessing. The congregation filed out of the church with the little angel's plea still singing in their ears: "Let Jesus show!"

The little angel's cry echoes that of John the Baptizer in today's gospel: "Behold, the Lamb of God." Behold, the Christ in your midst. May the little angel's cry be our prayer in the year ahead: "Let Jesus show!" in our homes and workplaces and schools; "Let Jesus show!" in our compassion, forgiveness, and joy. May we not "lose" Jesus in the many demands on our time; may we not "hide" Jesus when the difficult decision has to be made; may we not "pack" Jesus away until next Christmas—but may the "Word made flesh" make his dwelling place among us here, now and always, illuminating every one of our days with his wisdom and grace.

Meditation: What one image from this past Christmas would you like to see throughout the New Year?

Prayer: Lord God, may we behold your presence in every moment of this New Year. May you "show" in every act of kindness, in the most hidden work for justice and reconciliation, in every extended hand and heart to those in need.

The Spooky Old Woman at the Beach

Readings: 1 John 3:11-21; John 1:43-51

Scripture:
But Nathanael said to him,
   "Can anything good come from Nazareth?"
Philip said to him, "Come and see." (John 1:46)

Reflection: The children were having a great day at the beach riding the waves, building sand castles, playing Frisbee with Sweeney, the family canine.

In the distance an old woman appeared. Her tangle of gray hair fluttered; her clothes hung on her like tattered rags; her constant, indecipherable muttering buzzed above the sound of the surf as she bent down to pick up God-knows-what from the sand and then stuff whatever-it-is into her bag. As she approached, the parents instinctively moved toward their children, quietly instructing them to stay away from the strange woman. As she passed by, the old woman smiled at the family—but the smile was not returned.

After they left the beach, the father asked some local folks about the "spooky" old lady who had intruded on their day.

"Oh, that's Maggie," he was told. "She's a kind old soul. Every morning and afternoon she walks the beach picking up bits of glass and sharp stones and shells so children won't cut their feet."

Too often we gauge people according to our very dubious standards of who and what is good. The externals of dress, speech, and pedigree fail to take into account the true measure of an individual's worth: the love that is rooted in the human heart. We often reflect Nathanael's attitude: "Can anything good come from Nazareth?"

If we learn anything from the Christmas gospels, it is that God can be found in the most unexpected of places. God is present in the poverty of our Bethlehems, in the emptiness of our Nazareths, in the turmoil of our Bethsaidas. Whatever Nathanael-like biases and judgments we possess are shattered in the light of Christmas. God reveals himself in the generosity of a volunteer in a soup kitchen, in the patience of a teacher tutoring a struggling student, in the understanding of a high school senior who befriends the kid nobody else has time for. God's peace transforms our most challenging moments into occasions of grace; God's compassion illuminates our darkest nights with reason to hope and a sense of direction.

Often to our surprise, God seeks us out from our fig trees and invites us to realize a life transformed in Christ.

Meditation: Where have you unexpectedly found God?

Prayer: May the light of your grace illuminate our hearts, O God of compassion, dispelling the darkness of cynicism and opening our hearts to behold you in the most unexpected places. Open our eyes and hearts to behold your presence in every place, every moment, and every heart.

EPIPHANY AND
BAPTISM OF THE LORD

The Gifts of the Season

Readings: Isa 60:1-6; Eph 3:2-3a, 5-6; Matt 2:1-12

Scripture:
[The magi] opened their treasures
and offered him gifts of gold, frankincense, and myrrh.
(Matt 2:11)

Reflection: The gift-giving has mercifully come to an end.

For many of us, the most demanding part of Christmas shopping is deciding on the perfect gift, what best expresses our love and what will bring joy to those we love. Once we know the gift, the trek to the mall is considerably easier.

So what were the magi thinking? Did they just wrap up what they happened to have in their baggage (the first recorded instance of "re-gifting")? Were their gifts given with as much thought as a bottle of wine or a holiday fruitcake?

Or do the three gifts express something special about this Child that these men of learning perceived as a future king?

First, the gift of *gold*: Well, you can never go wrong with cash, right? But, in antiquity, gold was more than currency. The most valuable metal on earth, it was a symbol of divinity—the ultimate gift, the perfect offering to royalty. *This Child, who will be betrayed for silver, comes to transform our perspective of wealth to treasure again the things of God—compassion, forgiveness, and peace are the coin of the realm of the newborn King.*

Frankincense comes from a small tree found only in Arabia and northern Africa. The hardened resin of the plant was used as an all-purpose medicine: it was applied to stop bleeding and heal wounds; it was used as an antidote for poisons and a salve for bruises and ulcerations. *This Child comes to restore and heal not just the physical ailments of those he will meet in his gospel journey, but to heal humankind of our fears and doubts, to bridge the chasms that separate us from one another and from God.*

Myrrh was an expensive extract from the resin of the myrrh tree. It too was used as a medicine and, more significantly, in embalming the dead. Only the very wealthy and royalty were embalmed; myrrh, therefore, was a gift reserved for kings. *This Child comes to re-create us in the life of God: his death will be the defeat of death, his cross will be his—and our—glory.*

The three gifts of the magi are a gospel unto themselves. They honor the Child who is himself a gift from the God whose goodness knows neither limit nor condition. May we carry these gifts with us in the year ahead as we follow Christ the Morning Star on his journey to Jerusalem and beyond.

Meditation: What was the most satisfying and rewarding gift you *gave* this Christmas?

Prayer: O Christ, the very manifestation of God's love and radiance of the Father's light, illuminate the path we walk on our journey to God. May we come to your Father's dwelling place bearing the most precious of gifts we can possess: hearts transformed in your love, lives given over to your justice and reconciliation, spirits re-created in your peace.

January 7: Monday after Epiphany

"A Conspiracy of Goodness"

Readings: 1 John 3:22–4:6; Matt 4:12-17, 23-25

Scripture:
[Jesus] went around all of Galilee,
teaching in their synagogues,
proclaiming the Gospel of the Kingdom,
and curing every disease and illness among the people.
   (Matt 4:23)

Reflection: The parishioners of the small Protestant church of Le Chambon-sur-Lignon lived quiet, unnoticed lives as farmers and shopkeepers in their remote French mountain village. Then, at the outbreak of World War II, Jewish families began arriving at the small train station, seeking refuge from Nazi horrors. The French Vichy government, collaborators with the Germans, banned harboring Jewish refugees.

But the *Chambonnaise*, led by their pastor, defied the law and began offering refuge to any Jew who came to their village. Members of the little church took Jews into their homes, fed and clothed them, provided money and forged identification papers, and educated their children. Despite the growing suspicion of the French state police, the *Chambonnaise* managed to carry on their work in total secrecy. It is said that between 1940 and 1943, there was not a wine cellar or haystack or attic in all of Le Chambon that had not sheltered a Jewish child. At night, villagers would hide children in their wagons and transport them across the mountains to safety in Switzerland. It is estimated the *Chambonnaise* had saved more than five thousand Jews from the Holocaust.

An old villager later recalled, "It all happened very simply. We didn't ask ourselves why we were doing it. It was the human thing to do." When French government officials questioned the pastor, Andre Trocme, who led the work, Trocme defended his parish's actions: "These people came here for help and shelter. . . . We do not know what a Jew is. We only know men."

The story of Le Chambon mirrors Jesus' ministry of healing and teaching in Galilee. Pastor Trocme and the parishioners of Le Chambon provided the healing balm of hope and compassion to the Jews who have come to them for help; they proclaimed the justice and mercy of God in their quiet but brave defiance of the German and French governments.

In this hidden place, a village unnoticed by the rest of the world, the kingdom of God was proclaimed; from this unremarkable "Galilee" in the middle of the French Alps the great light of God shone.

Meditation: In what quiet, hidden ways can you bring healing and light to another?

Prayer: Lord Jesus, make us reflections of your light for those who have lost their way in the darkness of injustice and violence; may we bring healing and hope to the desperate and afraid through our compassion and care for them.

Sacred Vessels

Readings: 1 John 4:7-10; Mark 6:34-44

Scripture:
Then, taking the five loaves and the two fish and looking
   up to heaven,
   [Jesus] said the blessing, broke the loaves, and gave
      them to his disciples
   to set before the people;
   he also divided the two fish among them all. (Mark 6:41)

Reflection: The teacher asked her young students to bring to their next religious education class something that symbolized their families' faith. One student brought a rosary, another a Bible, a third a crucifix. But one brought perhaps the most meaningful expression of all: her mother's casserole dish.

In our church, we use many "sacred" vessels and objects in our worship: patens for the consecrated bread, chalices for the precious blood of the Lord, linens to cover the altar, thuribles of incense with clouds of smoke rising like our prayers to heaven.

But there are many other ordinary, common things we use every day that we would never think of as "sacred"—yet they can be instruments and tools of God's compassion.

For example, the Crock-Pot in which you make supper for a family in mourning is a sacred vessel. The towel you use to wipe the brow of a dying parent is as precious as altar linen. The soup kettle and ladle that are used to feed the poor and homeless transform a basement soup kitchen into a holy place. Every act of selfless generosity, every kindness extended, every moment given to the needs of another is the incense of prayer rising to God's dwelling place.

The early Christian community saw the feeding of the five thousand as a precursor to the Eucharist. Jesus challenges the Twelve to come up with whatever they can, if only a few pieces of fish and some scraps of bread. In doing so, Jesus forever connects compassion and generosity with the sacrament of his Body and Blood, just as he inextricably links the service of footwashing with the Eucharist at the Last Supper in the Fourth Gospel.

Jesus' gift of the Eucharist—the bread and wine blessed and broken for our sake—comes with an important string attached: it must be shared. In our taking the Body of Christ, we become the Body of Christ. In receiving the Eucharist, we must be willing to become Eucharist for others.

Meditation: What tool that you use every day can become a "sacred vessel" of Christ's compassion and peace?

Prayer: As you give to us, O God, may we give to one another. May our humble acts of generosity and forgiveness become visible signs of your invisible grace. Let our everyday efforts at reconciliation transform our simplest offerings into "sacred vessels" of your love. May we bless, break, and give from our own need in order to become Eucharist for others.

January 9: Wednesday after Epiphany

Learning to Swim

Readings: 1 John 4:11-18; Mark 6:45-52

Scripture:
"Take courage, it is I, do not be afraid!" (Mark 6:50)

Reflection: It was the six-year-old's first swimming lesson. His dad held him up as he got the rhythm of the stroke—hands gliding through the water and legs kicking to propel him forward. Dad waded alongside him—then slowly, imperceptibly, dad lowered his arms and let his son float. The six-year-old was swimming on his own.

He was doing well—until he looked over and saw that dad was no longer holding him up. He panicked and sank like a stone. Dad instantly pulled his son up out of the water and held him close until he coughed up the water. The little boy was shaken, but he trusted his dad to be there. Now, dad said, he had to trust himself to do it.

So father and son tried it again. When the novice swimmer got a good, even stroke going, his father slowly pulled away—and this time the boy continued on his own. He was swimming. And he knew it and he understood.

From now on, the six-year-old would always feel safe and secure in the water.

What happens to the young swimmer, what happens to the disciples in their wind-tossed skiff, happens to all of us at one time or another: we panic. We don't trust ourselves to know what the right thing is and our ability to do it. God reaches out and catches us, but we're not ready to risk giving up control and taking God's hand. Today's gospel challenges us to trust our understanding of discipleship and our heart's God-centered compass to live our baptism as disciples. Christ, in turn, promises to make his presence known to us, to hold us up and support us as we make our way through life's most turbulent waters.

Meditation: When have you experienced Christ calming a storm in your life in the compassion and support offered by another—and when have you been the calming presence of Christ's peace for someone?

Prayer: May we be your outreached hand to one another, O Lord. In embracing your spirit of peace and forgiveness, may we create in our homes and churches, our schools and businesses, safe harbors of understanding and support for everyone struggling to keep their heads above life's turbulent waters. In seeking to mirror your attitude of humility and selflessness, may we be a lifeline of support and trust for all who cry out to us for help.

January 10: Thursday after Epiphany

The Sign of Jonah

Readings: 1 John 4:19–5:4; Luke 4:14-22

Scripture:
The Spirit of the Lord is upon me,
  because he has anointed me
  to bring glad tidings to the poor. . . .
[Jesus] said to them,
  "Today this Scripture passage is fulfilled in your hearing."
(Luke 4:18, 21)

Reflection: Shortly after World War II, a Lutheran minister named Gunter Rutenborn staged a play called *The Sign of Jonah* that had a profound impact on the city of Berlin.

The play takes place in a Germany still reeling from the devastation of the war. A group of refugees are arguing as to who is responsible for the horror that has taken place. Some blame Hitler; others indict the munitions manufacturers; still others contend that the German people, in their apathy, bear responsibility for the destruction of their country.

As the debate reaches its climax, one of the plaintiffs makes a stunning indictment: God is culpable for what has happened. As Creator of this mad world, God is responsible for the insanity that has taken place. God should be called to justice for the pain the German people have suffered.

At first, everyone is stunned at the accusation, but gradually the chorus is picked up by all: "God is guilty! God is guilty! God is guilty!" And so God is put on trial for the crime of creation—and found guilty. The sentence: God is to be born a human being, poor and homeless, in scandal, deprived of rights. He will be surrounded by the sick, the filthy, the dying—he will know what it means to suffer and die. He will be misunderstood for the good he will try to do and condemned despite the righteousness of his life. And he will die in disgrace and be ridiculed. And three archangels are called down to execute the sentence. The play ends with the angels disappearing to carry out the sentence.

The audience who saw this extraordinary play and we who have encountered the Jesus of the gospels realize immediately that God has served his "sentence." God knows what it is like to live as a human being—which means that nothing we face today is unknown to God. The great message of the gospel is that God became what we are so that we can better understand what God is and what God is about: love, forgiveness, justice. Such is the "good news" of Jesus—God who empties himself of his divinity and enters human history, sanctifying humanity for all time.

Meditation: What facet of Jesus' "humanness" do you take most comfort in?

Prayer: With wonder and gratitude, O Lord, we behold your presence in our midst. In your suffering, may we learn persevering hope; in your poverty, may we understand what is of lasting value; in your death, may we learn the power of our crosses to bring forth life and resurrection into our lives and the lives of those we love.

Christmas Wishes

Readings: 1 John 5:5-13; Luke 5:12-16

Scripture:
[The leper] fell prostrate, pleaded with [Jesus], and said,
    "Lord, if you wish, you can make me clean."
Jesus stretched out his hand, touched him, and said,
    "I will do it. Be made clean." (Luke 5:12-13)

Reflection: Did you get everything you wanted and hoped for this Christmas?
    "If you wish . . ."
    As life gears up again after the Christmas holidays, what remains to be done? What did you want to do that got lost in the busyness of the holidays?
    "If you wish . . ."
    What resolution did you make for this New Year that has gotten off to a shaky start or has been lost altogether in the hard reality of every day?
    "If you wish . . ."
    The leper's words to Jesus resonate within our hearts and souls as we get down to the business and demands of 2013:
    If you wish, you can be reconciled with the family member or friend from whom you have been estranged . . .
    If you wish, you can bring change to an unjust or broken set of circumstances in your household or community . . .

If you wish, you can remove the stigma of "leprosy" from some-one's life; you can bring healing and consolation to a life broken with pain and grief; you can restore hope to someone who is lost and desperate.

The celebration of Jesus' birth is completed.

Now begins the work of Jesus.

"If you wish . . ."

Meditation: What one Christmas "wish" of yours remains unfulfilled? How can you bring it to fulfillment? What one resolution do you most hope to keep in the New Year? What are the major obstacles keeping you from realizing it?

Prayer: O healing Christ, remove the hopelessness that blinds us; cleanse us of the leprosy that divides us from others; and restore us to hope, that we may work in joy for the things we wish for most for ourselves and those we love.

Shepherds and Kings

Readings: 1 John 5:14-21; John 3:22-30

Scripture:
[John said:]
"The one who has the bride is the bridegroom;
the best man, who stands and listens for him,
rejoices greatly at the bridegroom's voice.
So this joy of mine has been made complete.
He must increase; I must decrease." (John 3:29-30)

Reflection: Every one of our lives is depicted in the Christmas gospels of Matthew and Luke.

Maybe you identify with the magi in the Epiphany story. Like the mysterious Eastern travelers, you search for meaning and purpose in your life; you seek something greater and more lasting than your profession or career. Follow the star to the Christ of selflessness and justice.

Or maybe you are a "shepherd," struggling to make a life for yourself and your family. You want your simple work and efforts to mean something. Embrace the angels' glad tidings. Come to Bethlehem and welcome the Christ who has come to re-create your life in the life of God.

There may be a Herod in you, so consumed with your pursuit of power and wealth that you destroy the dreams of anyone who gets in your way. Take off your crown, come down from your throne, and meet a king who possesses real power.

Maybe you are mired in the doubt of Zechariah, not daring to imagine the possibilities. Listen to the "Elizabeths" in your life; let them lead you to meaning and hope.

Remember that Mary and Joseph are your family too and that their Child is your newborn brother.

The Christmas and Epiphany stories we have read and celebrated over the past few weeks speak to all of us of a God who so loves the world he fashioned that he entered that world in the most humble and hidden way imaginable so that the world may be transformed in such love. Whether we are a shepherd or a king, whether we struggle in Bethlehem or move among the powerful in Jerusalem, God invites us to follow the star, to behold the Child in our stables, to let the holiness and compassion manifested in him illuminate our lives with joy and hope.

Meditation: What figure or character from the gospel stories of Jesus' birth do you especially identify with?

Prayer: As we stand at the beginning of this New Year, O God, we are humbled by the gift of yourself in the Child of Bethlehem. May your birth illuminate every day of this New Year; may the peace proclaimed by the angels resound in our own Bethlehems; may your star guide us on our journey in the seasons before us. Let your love bind us together as your sons and daughters, whether we are a shepherd or a king, a figure of power or a humble neighbor. By your grace help us to build your kingdom of peace and justice in every Bethlehem and Jerusalem.

The Holiness of a Drop of Water

Readings: Isa 40:1-5, 9-11; Titus 2:11-14; 3:4-7; Luke 3:15-16, 21-22

Scripture:
After all the people had been baptized
and Jesus also had been baptized and was praying,
heaven was opened and the Holy Spirit descended upon
   him
in bodily form like a dove.
And a voice came from heaven,
"You are my beloved Son; with you I am well pleased."
   (Luke 3:21-22)

Reflection: There is a beautiful Native American parable about the sacredness of water:

Father Sky gives to Mother Earth the clouds, which in turn are filled with water to nurture the good earth. A single raindrop falls on a meadow and joins other raindrops to become a trickle. The trickle becomes a stream and the stream becomes a river. The river then makes its way to the ocean, providing life-giving water to every creature and seedling along its way. The sun illuminates and warms the ocean, transforming some of its clear blue water into mist. The mist rises to Father Sky and becomes a cloud. And the cloud opens up and another raindrop falls to Mother Earth.

And another journey begins.

We are like raindrops, the ancients believed. We are all made from the same "holy stuff," the water that is life. In our time, our mothers give birth to us and we "fall" to earth. Each one of us is unique, each one of us possesses our own identity; but we are all part of what has gone before us and what comes after us. And, with other drops of rain, we journey to the same ocean and then back to Father Sky (adapted from *Soul Stories* by Gary Sukave).

In the waters of baptism, we begin our journey back to God, the Father who gives us this life in the first place. In these waters, we embrace the name of "Christ" and the Spirit of his gospel that unite us to the saints who have come before us and who will come after us. In these waters, we travel through life's deserts and meadows, in struggling trickles and powerful rivers to the ocean where one day we will "return" to God.

Baptism is not just a one-time rite of passage in our lives; it is an ongoing journey with God and to God, a sojourn across the waters to the dwelling place of the Father.

Meditation: How has this past Christmas renewed your understanding of being part of a family, a parish, a community?

Prayer: O God, in the waters of baptism you have raised us up and set us on our life's journey to your dwelling place. May the spring of your life within us make us currents of your reconciling and healing grace for all we travel with on this path to you.

References

December 7: Friday of the First Week of Advent
Charles Dickens, *A Christmas Carol*, ill. by Ronald Searle (London: Perpetua Books, 1961), 48, 49.

December 8: Immaculate Conception of the Blessed Virgin Mary
Bret Harte, "The Luck of Roaring Camp," in *Tales of the Gold Rush*, ill. by Fletcher Martin, intro. by Oscar Lewis (New York: Heritage Press, 1944), 3–15.

December 18: Tuesday in Late Advent
Ann Hood, "Holding a Little Girl's Hand," in *Dedicated to the People of Darfur: Writings on Fear, Risk, and Hope*, ed. Luke and Jennifer Reynolds (New Brunswick, NJ: Rutgers University Press, 2009), 17, 18.

December 19: Wednesday in Late Advent
Bernard Shaw, *Saint Joan*, in *Bernard Shaw's Plays*, ed. Warren S. Smith (New York: W.W. Norton, 1970), 190.

December 31: Seventh Day in the Octave of Christmas
Leslie Weatherhead, sermon cited in "God's Arms," by Michael Lindvall, *The Christian Century* (June 1, 2004).

January 2
Margaret Silf, "The Power of One," *America* (July 6–13, 2009).

January 4: Saint Elizabeth Ann Seton (Catholic Church)
Frederick Buechner, *Secrets in the Dark: A Life in Sermons* (San Francisco: HarperSanFrancisco, 2006), 268.

January 7: Monday after Epiphany

Pierre Sauvage, writer and director, *Weapons of the Spirit* (Pierre Sauvage Productions, 1988).

Philip Hallie, *Lest Innocent Blood Be Shed* (New York: Harper Colophon Books, 1979), 103.

January 10: Thursday after Epiphany

Guenter Tutenborn, *The Sign of Jonah: A Play in Nine Scenes*, trans. George White (Burien, WA: Dramatic Insights Publications, 2005).

January 13: The Baptism of the Lord

Gary Zukav, *Soul Stories* (New York: Fireside Books/Simon & Schuster, 2000), 51–52.